Sports Illustrated KIDS

LEGENDS IN THE MAKING

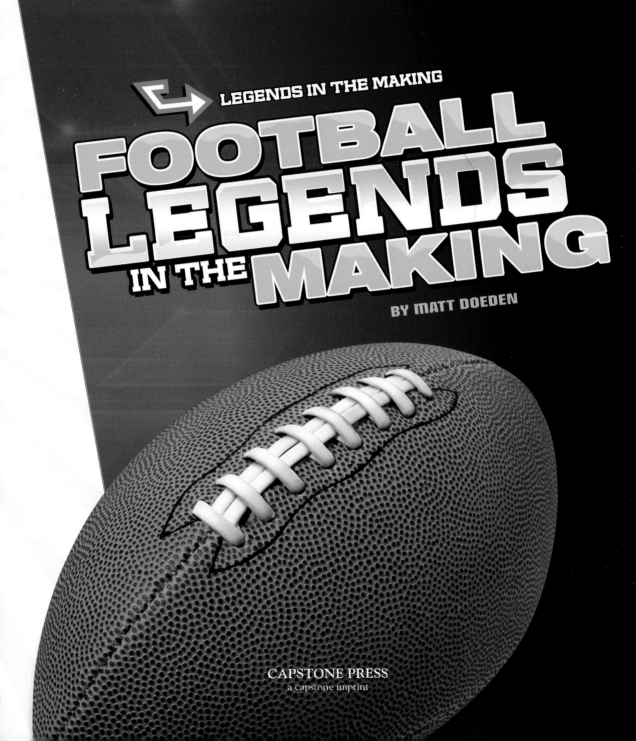

FOOTBALL LEGENDS IN THE MAKING

BY MATT DOEDEN

CAPSTONE PRESS
a capstone imprint

Sports Illustrated Kids Legends in the Making are published by Capstone Press, 1710 Roe Crest Drive, North Mankato, Minnesota 56003
www.capstonepub.com

Library of Congress Cataloging-in-Publication Data
Doeden, Matt.
  Football legends in the making / by Matt Doeden.
      pages cm.—(Sports illustrated kids. Legends in the making)
  Includes index.
  ISBN 978-1-4765-4064-1 (library binding)
  ISBN 978-1-4765-5190-6 (paperback)
1. Football players—Biography—Juvenile literature. I. Title.
  GV939.A1D64 2014
  796.3320922—dc23   2013032773

Editorial Credits
Anthony Wacholtz, editor; Ted Williams, set designer; Terri Poburka, designer; Eric Gohl, media researcher; Jennifer Walker, production specialist

Photo Credits
Newscom: ZUMA Press/Gene Lower, 20; Shutterstock: Lightspring, 1; *Sports Illustrated*: Al Tielemans, cover (bottom left), 16, 26–27 (bkg), 27, 31, Bill Frakes, 23, Bob Rosato, 7, 8–9 (bkg), Damian Strohmeyer, 12, 16–17 (bkg), 19, 24, David E. Klutho, 4, 4–5 (bkg), 14–15 (bkg), 28–29 (bkg), 30 (bottom), John Biever, 8, 10–11 (bkg), 11, 12–13 (bkg), 28, John W. McDonough, cover (bottom right), 15, 22–23 (bkg), Peter Read Miller, 20–21 (bkg), 24–25 (bkg), Simon Bruty, cover (top), 6–7 (bkg), 18–19 (bkg), 30 (top)

Design Elements
Shutterstock

Printed in the United States of America in Stevens Point, Wisconsin.
092013   007768WZS14

TABLE OF CONTENTS

. . . . 4
CALVIN JOHNSON 6
MATT RYAN 9
CLAY MATTHEWS 10
A.J. GREEN 13
ADRIAN PETERSON 14
J.J. WATT 17
RAY RICE 18
JULIO JONES 21
PATRICK PETERSON 22
MATTHEW STAFFORD 25
ROB GRONKOWSKI 26
LeSEAN McCOY 29
ARIAN FOSTER 30
RISING STARS 32
READ MORE 32
INTERNET SITES 32
INDEX . . . .

Fans love to watch their favorite National Football League (NFL) players pass, run, and hit. Legends such as Joe Montana and Barry Sanders have helped make pro football so popular. Which of today's up-and-coming stars are on their way to greatness? Turn the page to learn more about some of the league's most talented players.

CALVIN JOHNSON

POSITION:
WIDE RECEIVER

HEIGHT:	WEIGHT:
6 FEET 5 INCHES (196 CM)	236 POUNDS (107 KG)

COLLEGE:
GEORGIA TECH

NFL TEAM:
DETROIT LIONS

Calvin Johnson is one of the most talented wide receivers in NFL history. He's tall, strong, fast, and has amazing hands. All a quarterback needs to do is get the ball close, and Johnson can do the rest. He's almost impossible to defend with just one player.

Johnson was a star receiver at Georgia Tech. He won the 2006 Biletnikoff Award as the best receiver in college football. After joining the Detroit Lions in 2007, he became an instant NFL star. His 12 receiving touchdowns in 2008 led the league. In 2012 he gained 1,964 receiving yards, shattering the single-season record by more than 100 yards.

Johnson is a three-time **All Pro**. If he can stay healthy, he may one day challenge Jerry Rice's all-time record for career receiving yards.

Did You Know?

Johnson's nickname is Megatron. A teammate gave him the name because Johnson reminded him of the popular Transformers character.

ALL PRO—an honor given to players voted the league's best player at their position

"Matty Ice" gets his nickname for his ability to remain cool and calm under pressure. Ryan is a classic **pocket passer**, with a cannon for an arm. He's great at throwing **timing routes**, but he can also chuck long bombs down the field.

Ryan took over as the Atlanta Falcons' starter in 2008. He was named the NFL's offensive Rookie of the Year and led Atlanta to the playoffs. Ryan has gotten even better since then, including an amazing season in 2012. He threw for a career-high 4,719 yards and 32 touchdowns. He also led the NFL by completing 68.6 percent of his passes.

After the 2012 season, Ryan led the Falcons to their first playoff victory since 2004. If he continues to improve, he may one day lead them to the Super Bowl.

⤷ Did You Know?

Ryan is also an excellent golfer. During the off-season he takes part in charity golf tournaments.

POCKET PASSER—a quarterback who usually stays behind his line in the pocket, rarely running the ball

TIMING ROUTE—a passing play that relies on precise timing by the passer and receiver

MATT RYAN

POSITION:
QUARTERBACK

HEIGHT:	WEIGHT:
6 FEET 4 INCHES (193 CM)	217 POUNDS (98 KG)

COLLEGE:
BOSTON COLLEGE

NFL TEAM:
ATLANTA FALCONS

CLAY MATTHEWS

POSITION:
LINEBACKER

HEIGHT:
6 FEET 3 INCHES
(191 CM)

WEIGHT:
255 POUNDS
(116 KG)

COLLEGE:
UNIVERSITY OF
SOUTHERN CALIFORNIA

NFL TEAM:
GREEN BAY PACKERS

Green Bay Packers linebacker Clay Matthews is one of the most explosive defenders in the NFL. His size and speed make him a one-man wrecking crew. He can blast through opposing blockers or speed around them. He's also an excellent tackler. It's hard for the ballcarrier to break free when Matthews makes contact.

The Packers selected Matthews in the 2009 NFL draft. He made an instant impact. Matthews had 10 sacks as a rookie and earned a spot at the Pro Bowl. In 2010 he was named the National Football Conference (NFC) Defensive Player of the Year. He also forced a key fumble in the Packers' Super Bowl victory that season.

Matthews faces a lot of **double teams**, so the Packers line him up all over the field. That allows him to make more plays and earn his nickname, the Claymaker.

Did You Know?

Matthews has football in his family. His grandfather, father, and uncle all played in the NFL.

DOUBLE TEAM—the strategy of using two players to block or cover one opponent

A.J. Green of the Cincinnati Bengals is the total package. The wide receiver has the speed to burn past defenders. He's tall and has long arms, providing a big target to his quarterback. He has the hands to catch almost anything that comes his way. Put it all together and you've got one of the most dangerous receivers in the league.

Green had a solid college career at the University of Georgia before joining the Bengals in 2011. During his NFL rookie year he tallied more than 1,000 receiving yards and made the Pro Bowl. Green followed with an even better 2012. He piled up 1,350 receiving yards and 11 touchdowns while earning a second straight Pro Bowl invitation.

⇨ Did You Know?

Green was on his elementary school's juggling team. He says that juggling helped build his hand-eye coordination.

A.J. GREEN

POSITION:
WIDE RECEIVER

HEIGHT:	WEIGHT:
6 FEET 4 INCHES (193 CM)	207 POUNDS (94 KG)

COLLEGE:
UNIVERSITY OF GEORGIA

NFL TEAM:
CINCINNATI BENGALS

ADRIAN PETERSON

POSITION:

RUNNING BACK

HEIGHT:	WEIGHT:
6 FEET 1 INCH (185 CM)	217 POUNDS (98 KG)

COLLEGE:
UNIVERSITY OF OKLAHOMA

NFL TEAM:
MINNESOTA VIKINGS

Adrian Peterson is one of the most physical runners in the game. The Minnesota Vikings running back has a rare combination of speed and power. He can bash into tacklers, throw them aside, or just use his breakaway speed to burn past them. He doesn't avoid contact—he takes the punishment to the defense.

A.P. came into the league with a bang in 2007. In just his eighth NFL game, he rushed for 296 yards and broke the single-game rushing record. He won the NFL rushing title in 2008 with 1,760 yards.

Peterson suffered a terrible knee injury late in 2011. Some thought his career was over. But Peterson was better than ever in 2012. He rushed for 2,097 yards, the second-highest total in NFL history. Peterson carried the Vikings into the playoffs and was named league MVP.

⤷ Did You Know?

Peterson's dad gave him the nickname All Day because he never stops going.

J.J. Watt is a quarterback's worst nightmare. The Houston Texans defensive end uses his speed and quickness to slide past blockers and sack the quarterback. If he can't do that, he gets his hands in the air to bat down passes.

Watt started out as a tight end. But while in college at the University of Wisconsin, he switched to defense. It was a good move. The Texans picked Watt in the first round of the 2011 NFL Draft, and he quickly became a force in the league. His 2012 season was one of a kind. He had 20.5 sacks and broke up 16 passes. No player in NFL history had ever had 15 or more sacks and passes defended in a season. He was named Defensive Player of the Year and led the Texans to the playoffs.

⤷ Did You Know?

As a teenager Watt was also a star player in baseball, basketball, track, and hockey.

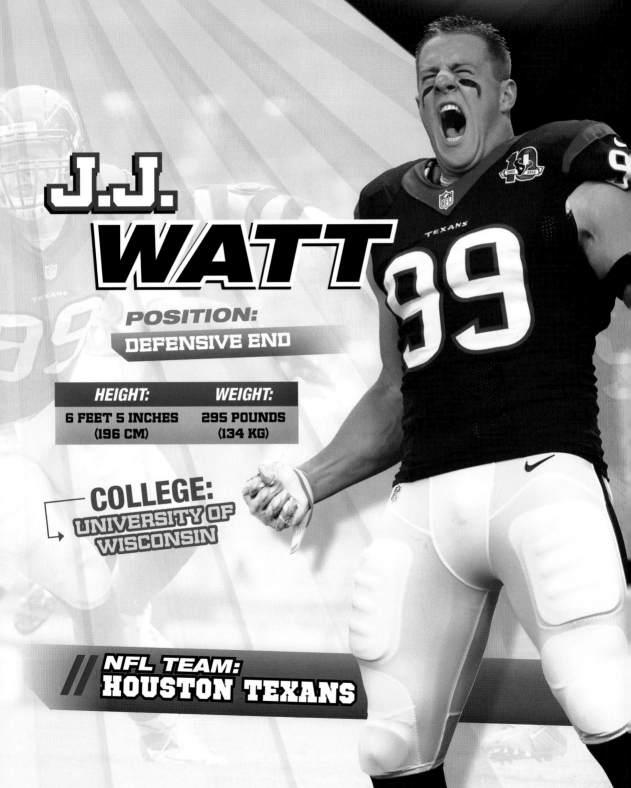

J.J. WATT

POSITION:
DEFENSIVE END

HEIGHT:	WEIGHT:
6 FEET 5 INCHES (196 CM)	295 POUNDS (134 KG)

COLLEGE:
UNIVERSITY OF WISCONSIN

NFL TEAM:
HOUSTON TEXANS

RAY RICE

POSITION:

RUNNING BACK

HEIGHT:	WEIGHT:
5 FEET 9 INCHES (175 CM)	195 POUNDS (88 KG)

COLLEGE:

 RUTGERS

NFL TEAM:
BALTIMORE RAVENS

Ray Rice is the ultimate **all-purpose** back. He's a tough, fast runner with excellent hands to catch passes. He can burn opposing defenses on the ground or through the air. That makes him one of the league's most dangerous weapons.

Rice was not a highly ranked prospect coming out of Rutgers in 2008. Some thought he was too small to be the main running back. But the Ravens picked Rice in the second round. He was Baltimore's backup running back as a rookie. He became the starter in 2009 and instantly became one of the NFL's best. In 2011 he led the NFL with 2,068 **yards from scrimmage**. In 2012 he helped the Ravens win a Super Bowl.

Did You Know?

Rice's daughter is named Rayven.

ALL-PURPOSE—describes a player who excels in both the running and passing game

YARDS FROM SCRIMMAGE—a players' combined rushing and receiving yards

Julio Jones is the perfect deep-ball target. The wide receiver's size and speed allow him to get downfield and outleap defenders. Jones also has some of the best hands in the league. If he can reach the ball, he can catch it. His skills make him a powerful offensive weapon.

Jones had a great college career at the University of Alabama. He helped the Crimson Tide go 14-0 and win the national championship after the 2009 season. The Falcons selected him in the first round of the 2011 NFL Draft. Jones proved he was ready as a rookie, averaging 17.8 yards per catch. He was even better in 2012. He collected 1,198 receiving yards and 10 touchdowns. Jones helped the Falcons reach the playoffs and was named to his first Pro Bowl.

⇨ Did You Know?

Jones' given name is Quintorris Lopez Jones. Julio has always been his nickname.

JULIO JONES

POSITION:
WIDE RECEIVER

HEIGHT:	WEIGHT:
6 FEET 3 INCHES (191 CM)	220 POUNDS (100 KG)

COLLEGE:
UNIVERSITY OF ALABAMA

NFL TEAM:
ATLANTA FALCONS

PATRICK PETERSON

POSITION:
CORNERBACK, PUNT RETURNER

HEIGHT:	**WEIGHT:**
6 FEET (183 CM)	219 POUNDS (99 KG)

COLLEGE:
LOUISIANA STATE UNIVERSITY

NFL TEAM:
ARIZONA CARDINALS

Patrick Peterson is a true double threat. He's one of the game's top cornerbacks, and he's one of the best punt returners in the league. His speed and athletic ability make him a threat all over the field. He can even play wide receiver.

Peterson was a star at Louisiana State University. In 2010 he won the Chuck Bednarik Award as college football's best defensive player. The Cardinals picked him fifth in the 2011 draft. Peterson made an instant impact for the defense. But he really shined returning punts. He tied a record with four punt returns for touchdowns in 2011. In 2012 Peterson stepped up as one of the league's best cornerbacks. He led the Cardinals with seven interceptions. He also led the NFL with five fumble recoveries.

Did You Know?

In 2011 Peterson dropped back to field a punt in an overtime game against the Rams. He caught the ball at his own 1-yard line. Then he darted 99 yards for a touchdown that ended the game!

The Detroit Lions' Matthew Stafford is a one-of-a-kind quarterback. Most star NFL quarterbacks have one set throwing motion, but not Stafford. The young star is famous for having many ways of delivering a pass. He throws overhand, sidearm, underhand—whatever it takes. Stafford also throws one of the best deep balls in the game.

The Lions picked Stafford first overall in the 2009 NFL Draft. Stafford struggled with injuries early in his career. But since 2011 he's been a passing machine. In 2011 he became just the fourth quarterback in history to throw for 5,000 or more yards in a single season. He also threw 41 touchdown passes. In 2012 he set an NFL record by attempting 727 passes.

⤳ Did You Know?

In 2009 Stafford threw five touchdowns in a single game—the most ever by a rookie.

MATTHEW STAFFORD

POSITION:

QUARTERBACK

HEIGHT:	WEIGHT:
6 FEET 2 INCHES (188 CM)	232 POUNDS (105 KG)

COLLEGE:
UNIVERSITY OF GEORGIA

NFL TEAM:
DETROIT LIONS

ROB
GRONKOWSKI

POSITION:

TIGHT END

HEIGHT:	WEIGHT:
6 FEET 6 INCHES (198 CM)	265 POUNDS (120 KG)

COLLEGE:
UNIVERSITY OF ARIZONA

NFL TEAM:
NEW ENGLAND PATRIOTS

Rob Gronkowski is quickly becoming one of the best pass-catching tight ends in football history. He has it all. He's an excellent route-runner, and he uses his big body and soft hands to snatch balls out of the air. That makes him a perfect target in the New England Patriots offense.

"Gronk" was a standout in college at the University of Arizona before the Patriots drafted him in 2010. He showed early that he knew how to reach the end zone. He scored 10 touchdowns as a rookie. Then in 2011 he had the greatest season any tight end has ever had. He collected 1,327 receiving yards and had 17 touchdown catches. Both were the most ever for a tight end. Injuries slowed him down in 2012, but he still managed 11 touchdowns in 11 games.

⟜ Did You Know?

In 2011 Gronkowski became the first tight end to lead the NFL in touchdown catches.

Philadelphia running back LeSean McCoy is a threat every time he touches the ball. His quick feet and blazing speed make him one of the league's most explosive runners. And he's just as dangerous catching passes.

McCoy rushed for 35 touchdowns in just two college seasons at the University of Pittsburgh. But his small size scared off some NFL teams. He wasn't picked until the second round of the 2009 NFL Draft. McCoy quickly proved that he could make it in the NFL. In 2011 he led the league with 17 rushing touchdowns. He also made his first Pro Bowl appearance. Experts believe that if McCoy can stay healthy, there will be many successful seasons to come.

⤷ Did You Know?

McCoy organized a foundation called Shades of Greatness. The foundation raises money for Lou Gehrig's disease research.

LeSEAN McCOY

POSITION:
RUNNING BACK

HEIGHT:	**WEIGHT:**
5 FEET 10 INCHES (178 CM)	215 POUNDS (98 KG)

COLLEGE:
UNIVERSITY OF PITTSBURGH

NFL TEAM:
PHILADELPHIA EAGLES

ARIAN FOSTER

POSITION:
RUNNING BACK

HEIGHT:	WEIGHT:
6 FEET 1 INCH (185 CM)	228 POUNDS (103 KG)

COLLEGE:
UNIVERSITY OF TENNESSEE

NFL TEAM:
HOUSTON TEXANS

Houston Texans running back Arian Foster isn't the biggest or the fastest runner in the NFL. But he may be one of the smartest and most patient. Foster relies on his great vision and ability to hit the right hole at the right time. Foster is also a great pass-catcher and a reliable blocker.

Foster was not a big prospect coming out of the University of Tennessee in 2009. Nobody picked him during the NFL Draft. Foster signed with Houston as a **free agent**. Houston cut him at one point, but he later rejoined the team. He barely played as a rookie, but in 2010 he got his chance. He led the NFL with 1,616 rushing yards and 16 rushing touchdowns. Since then he's remained one of the game's top backs. He's already the Texans' all-time leading rusher, and he's been to three Pro Bowls.

➲ Did You Know?

Foster does a bow after every touchdown he scores. He says he bows to give respect to the game he loves.

FREE AGENT—a player who is free to sign with any team

RISING STARS

ROBERT GRIFFIN III

Washington Redskins quarterback RGIII electrified fans in 2012 with his ability to run and throw.

LUKE KUECHLY

Carolina linebacker Luke Kuechly is a tackling machine. He led the league with 164 tackles as a rookie in 2012 and was named Defensive Rookie of the Year.

ANDREW LUCK

The top overall pick of the 2012 NFL Draft, Luck is a pure pocket passer. The Indianapolis Colts quarterback combines a rocket arm with great accuracy and poise under pressure.

DOUG MARTIN

Tampa Bay Buccaneers running back Doug Martin is a threat to take it all the way every time he touches the ball. In 2012 Martin tied a record by rushing for four touchdowns in a half.

CAM NEWTON ⇨

The first pick in the 2011 NFL Draft ran and threw his way to the Offensive Rookie of the Year award with the Carolina Panthers.

BLAIR WALSH

Minnesota Vikings kicker Blair Walsh was the league's top kicker as a rookie in 2012. He set an NFL record by making nine field goals of 50 or more yards.

READ MORE

Doeden, Matt. *The World's Greatest Football Players.* Sports Illustrated Kids. Mankato, Minn.: Capstone Press, 2010.

Savage, Jeff. *Calvin Johnson.* Minneapolis: Lerner Publications Company, 2013.

Schuh, Mari C. *Adrian Peterson.* New York: Bearport Pub., 2013.

INTERNET SITES

FactHound offers a safe, fun way to find Internet sites related to this book. All of the sites on FactHound have been researched by our staff.

Here's all you do:

Visit *www.facthound.com*

Type in this code: 9781476540641

Super-cool stuff! Check out projects, games and lots more at **www.capstonekids.com**

INDEX

awards, 5, 6, 9, 13, 14, 21, 30, 31
cornerbacks, 21
defensive ends, 14
kickers, 31
linebackers, 9, 30
nicknames, 5, 6, 13, 18, 25, 30

punt returners, 21
quarterbacks, 6, 22, 30, 31
running backs, 13, 17, 26, 29, 31
tight ends, 25
wide receivers, 5, 10, 18